A little book on finding your Way:
Zen and the Art of Doing stuff

Also by Francis Briers:

My Tao Te Ching: A Fool's Guide to Effing the Ineffable

The Spiritual Development Activity Book

Somatic Presence Coaching: An approach to educating the body

The Shapes of my Yearning – a poetry collection

A little book on finding your Way:

Zen and the Art of Doing stuff

By Francis Briers

Warriors of Love Publishing

ISBN 978-0-9567799-0-8

A copy of this book has been deposited with the British Library.

Published by Warriors of Love (WOL) Publishing

Contents

Introduction: The Way 6

Chapter 1: All Zen Masters are Geeks and Anoraks! 9

Chapter 2: Principles 13

Question Set 1: Finding your Way 16

Chapter 3: Philosophy 19

Question Set 2: Finding your Philosophy 31

Chapter 4: Form 33

Question Set 3: Finding your Form 57

Chapter 5: Practice 59

Closing words: Short book, long path 75

Appendices 76
Principles and Question Sets 77
Guidelines for interviewing and forming a group 83
Resources 88
Acknowledgements 89
Author Profile 90

Introduction: The Way

We all want to be good at something. Let's face it, most of us who haven't had all the passion squeezed out of us want to be <u>really</u> good at something. It almost doesn't matter what the thing is – just to be that good, to be able to say "I'm World-class." But how do we envision this goal? I'd say that in the western world we have a pretty limited idea of what achievement really means. It mostly seems to mean Bigger, Faster, Stronger, Taller, just plain MORE! I think there's another way...

It's a way that has been around in the West forever but has only been applied to certain disciplines (primarily the arts). It has been suggested by certain modern and progressive psychologies. But I think it has been best explored and expressed in the Far East where it has been inherent in some of their oldest philosophical approaches. What is that way? Good question.

It is **The *Way.*** It has it's roots in Taoism (an ancient Chinese religion and spiritual path) and found further expression in Japanese Zen Buddhism. *'Tao'* (sometimes *Dao*) in Chinese or *'Do'* in Japanese translates as *'Way.'* So when I say it's The *Way*, that's what I mean – The *Way* as in The *Tao*, or The *Do*. *'The Way'* in Taoism and the *Do*-forms in Japan are practices like martial arts, or calligraphy, or brush-painting but they are much more than just an activity, they are the medium through which the practitioner meditates, explores the nature of the universe, and creates the most fundamental expression of how they live their life! These are not just hobbies, they are life practices. I think, if the ancient Chinese could turn flower-arranging into a *Way*, then why not turn anything into a *Way*? So this book is not just about doing stuff it's about *Do*-ing stuff: taking something you **do** and making it a ***Do*** (see how beautifully I've set up that pun? That's part of my *Way*, I learnt it from my Dad).

The *Way* is not about Bigger, Faster, Stronger, Taller or More. It is about someone expressing their essential nature. It is about blossoming into the fullness of your being – and not in an 'I'm the most beautiful blossom ever' kinda way – in a 'finding out who you are and living that' kinda way. When you really do that, as the song says, nobody does it better.

This is not about converting you to some religion, making you shave your head, selling you a line of 'The *Way*'™ T-shirts, or selling your Soul to Santa. It could be described as a spiritual path but only in so much as it is a path and if you want to you can involve your spiritual self in the journey. That's all up to you. My personal experience is that by taking certain activities and bringing a special mindset to them I have learned about myself and found a deeper sense of who I really am. It's not any kind of objective truth (if such a thing exists) but it has brought me joy in the good times and peace in the tough times and that's good enough for me.

The *Way* is not really about the activities that help to cultivate it. The *Way* is your unique path in the world. When that's really written in your heart then you can experience all kinds of *Ways* and all kinds of people and they all help to feed you in your own *Way*. In the words of the Hagakure[1]:

"It is bad when one thing becomes two. One should not look for anything else in the Way of the Samurai. It is the same for anything that is called a Way. Therefore it is inconsistent to hear something of the Way of Confucius or the Way of the Buddha, and say that this is the Way of the Samurai. If one understands things in this manner, he should be able to hear about all Ways and be more and more in accord with his own."

For this reason I think anything can be a *Way*. That's what this book is about – helping you to find an activity you love enough to really work at it and then developing it into a *Way*.

---

1 Hagakure, The Book of the Samurai by Yamamoto Tsunetomo, Translated by William Scott Wilson

Chapter 1: All Zen Masters are Geeks and Anoraks![2]

I think one of the reasons why we view mastery and excellence as we do in the West is because of school: In school it's not cool to be good at stuff unless it's mainstream. This will probably depend on the school but at my school, being good at football was cool. Sports were generally a cool thing to be good at but Football was top of the pile. Music might be cool to be good at... guitar was cool, oboe was not. As we got older and moved towards driving age, knowing a lot about cars was cool. Being academically strong was not cool, but particularly maths, the sciences and history were not cool. Religious Studies didn't even get on the radar. These are mostly examples from the boys side of the fence and from my school in particular but most of us develop a sixth sense about what's cool and what's not when we are at school and I'm sure you can fill in your own examples.

In this environment where only certain activities are safe to be enthusiastic about, is it any wonder that many of us loose our way? In the rarefied social environment of

---

2 Since first starting to work on this book it has come to my attention that people outside of the UK have no idea what 'Anorak' means! So, to explain: an anorak is technically speaking a type of water-proof jacket – maybe like a wind-cheater in the US? However, when applied as a label for a person it indicates that they are passionately, almost obsessively interested in something which involves a high degree of technical knowledge. Usually it is something which is not cool to like, let alone love. In the UK a train-spotter or stamp-collector might be seen as an 'Anorak.' A pop-culture reference could be the character Ross from 'Friends' and how he's always correcting people about obscure details to do with dinosaurs. Hope that helps!

the playground or the sports field or the canteen you just didn't say "You know what? I love Renaissance poetry!" If you did you were a geek. Likewise, it would have been a special kind of social suicide to say "This algebra stuff is brilliant, I could just play with numbers and letters like this all day!" If you did you were an anorak.

Most of us will have had relatively little safe space growing up to explore what really excited us. We have been socially educated to hide away any passions which don't 'fit the mould' of our peer group.

I think that to find our *Way* we have to love something. It's not always the case but I've often found that the things I fall in love with are things I have some natural talent for. That doesn't mean I find them easy – the challenge is part of what gets me really hooked long-term – but when I first try it there's a zing of recognition like I've done it before and the process of learning is more like a 'remembering'.

I never really learnt to love football, but it wouldn't surprise me if many of my school friends did. They learnt to love it but I suspect only a handful loved it straight away. In my heart there were other things I loved straight away, and some of them have taken years to discover. Most of the things I love would have definitely placed me in the Geek-camp at school. Karate was one of them, but not the high kicking, cool 'Karate Kid' Karate, no.... A rare form of old Okinawan Karate that is compact and probably not that impressive to watch. Another example would be a love of world religions and philosophies. Definitely not cool where I came from. My most recent discovery is 'Card Scaling'. "What is that?!" I hear you cry. It is the skill of throwing playing cards with enough power to stick in a water-melon or fly for hundreds of feet. Throwing playing cards like a ninja! Sound kinda geeky? Fair enough, but I love it.

It is interesting to note how people in the East who obsessively train in obscure disciplines are given titles of respect, while in the West they are called Geeks and Anoraks. Take a Zen master as an example. He (or she) spends years sitting still. Their other key activity is contemplating ancient pieces of short and confusing poetry. It sounds like a geek and smells like a geek, it's a geek! Ancient poetry that doesn't have any immediate or obvious meaning?! What an anorak!

If you want to master something, if you want to find a *Way* that will nourish you and help you grow it's got to be something that lives in your heart; and that means that, by the world's standards, it might not be cool.

There are *Ways* already defined and laid out for you to pick up: the martial arts, zen flower arranging, calligraphy, brush painting, pottery, carving, the Japanese tea ceremony. That's not what this book is about. What I'm looking to do here is set out some principles so that you can take any activity and turn it into a *Way*. Hell, if the Samurai and monks of ancient Japan could turn making the tea into a Zen art then why shouldn't we be able to do the same with anything? Wine tasting is virtually there already but it could be anything: Cake baking, accountancy, the application of make-up, dog walking, throwing stones into the sea – anything!

If you're going to undertake this task and find a *Way* for yourself you'd better get in touch with your inner geek. Revere the anorak in your heart. These are the parts of you that are capable of completely investing themselves in the deep, deep detail of their activities no matter what anyone else thinks. And remember that all Zen masters are Geeks and Anoraks.

Some of you who have an altruistic outlook and want to take care of others or even change the world may be wondering if this isn't all a bit self serving. Isn't it a bit selfish to dig deep into myself and find what I like to do and really invest time in it, regardless of whether it is an activity that serves others? I would say no. If you don't take care of the vessel doing the work (that's you) then the work won't get done. One of my favourite quotes at the moment is this one from Howard Thurman:

"Don't ask yourself what the world needs; ask yourself what makes you come alive. And then go and do that. Because what the world needs is people who have come alive."

Chapter 2: Principles

As I have mentioned above, in this book I am looking to offer some core principles for developing something you do into a *Do* or *Way*. This really could be any activity. I would recommend something that you feel a natural pull towards, and probably something you have some basic talent for – although that doesn't have to be the case. It needs to be something that you can continue to grow within and refine but don't get too hung-up on this. The principles I am going to lay out here will, I believe, add layers of depth to any activity.

I wanted to keep it simple to remember so there are just three principles. By the nature of them being principles there is a fair amount of depth and richness of detail to each, but nonetheless there are only three to remember. The beauty of it is that the principles will help you to deepen into your *Way*, and as that happens you will gain more insight into the principles. Pretty cool huh?

So, the principles are.....

Philosophy

Your *Way* needs to have a stated philosophy – a yardstick against which attitude, thought and action are measured

Form

Your *Way* needs to have ritual forms which clearly denote when you are engaged in practice. These signal to your psyche that something special is going on.

Practice

You have to practice your *Way*. That's how it works. If you are not doing it then the *Way* is just an idea, rather than a *Way*.

In the coming chapters I will expand on each of these principles and equip you with a sufficient sense of what these principles are and why they are vital in pursuing a *Do* rather than just doing something. If any of my ideas don't work for you, that's fine, these aren't rules you have to follow, they are guidelines. However, I would recommend you try stuff out before you discard it. Some things only come alive when they are taken into action.

For some of you it may be the case that you feel drawn to developing a *Way* but don't know where to start. What doing will you make into a *Do*-ing? Well, I can't tell you that. You can try a few different things out, it may behove you to try one of the established forms to get a feel for the thing, or you can just start asking yourself some questions. You can even get a friend to help you so that <u>they</u> ask the questions – it can make it easier to muddle through the answers and may have the added bonus of deepening your friendship (there's some guidelines for how to do this interviewing process after the questions). Now there's something I may be able to help you with. I can suggest some useful questions. So, here goes...

Question set 1: Finding your *Way*

a) What do you love doing? (don't count anything out, remember, I throw playing cards across the room).

b) You know that feeling you get where you are at your most alive, awake and alert – not from a rush of adrenalin but with a wholesome, satisfied deep breath and big smile kind of feeling? What are you doing when you feel like that?

c) Is there an activity which is difficult but you keep going back to it nonetheless because it's juicy, deepening and strangely satisfying?

d) What do you read up about, find websites about, study for and ponder even though it's not your job?

e) Is there an activity where you feel at home, like this is the thing you were born to do – that doesn't mean it's easy or that you're the best at it: It just feels right.

If you're working together with someone else as an 'interviewer' (and I'd really recommend it – the conversations we have are the way we shape our world) then I offer here some guidelines for the interviewer:

1. It is your job to hear the story, not tell it – just listen.

2. If you hear something that intuitively makes your ears prick up: ask to hear more about it.

3. Take a few notes as you're listening. It will help you both to spot patterns, and where there's a pattern, there may be a Way.

4. Listen with an open heart – try not to judge what you hear, empathise with your partner in *Do*-ing.

5. Cultivate an attitude of fascination. One of my teachers, a wonderful lady called Jane Magruder-Watkins, has this great way of saying "Isn't that interesting..." She really means it and the way she says it makes you reconsider what you've just said and become fascinated in it yourself. That's what you're after (and don't give yourself a hard time if you don't quite get it, Jane's had a lot of practice).

Philosophy

Chapter 3: Philosophy

In the immortal words of the truly wonderful songwriter Ben Folds:

"I don't care you can say what you want to, I've got my philosophy! (keeps my feet on the ground)"[3]

Whether we intend to or not we all have a philosophy already. It's our outlook on the world, the beliefs we hold about life, and the yardstick against which we measure our actions (and, if we're being judgemental, other people's actions as well). Much of our internal philosophy will be unconsidered, unconscious and often learnt from our parents, or peers. We either swallow it whole or we spot it, don't like it, and then try and do the opposite. Now, I don't think it's a bad idea to get a little more conscious about what your philosophy is full stop, but when it comes to developing a *Way* we definitely need to make the philosophy a conscious one. I'm not saying it's all got to be totally definable and written down – some of the best things in life can't be defined in so limited a form – but you've got to know it in yourself even if that just means having a clear feeling for it in your heart.

All of the traditional *Ways* in the East and West have a philosophy. They might not call it that – if it's an art form they might call it an aesthetic – but it's much the

---

3   It's in his song 'Philosophy' which is an awesome song, best heard on his 'Ben Folds Live' album

same thing in terms of its function. The philosophy of the practice is what shapes the form of the practice and defines what it is you are trying to <u>refine</u> in yourself by <u>doing</u> the practice. It's the answer to the question "Why are you doing what you're doing?"

Hopefully you're starting to see why the philosophy is important in finding your *Way*. Without it you are waiving your arms about in the dark, blindly fumbling your way – you don't know why - towards something – you don't know what. Is it any wonder so many people feel lost and afraid for so much of their lives?! Now I'm not saying that a philosophy is the heal-all of our modern culture, but I think it helps to have a sense of purpose. Unless you want to go to a very dogmatic religion and have someone else tell you what the point of your life should be (more of that 'swallowing stuff whole') then you're going to need to make some decisions about what you <u>want</u> the point of your life to be. Religions can often offer useful frameworks and guidance, but with most, you're still going to have to find your own interpretation of what the divine poetry really means.

So, one of the purposes of a philosophy is to give a purpose to what we choose to spend our time doing (or *Do*-ing) but it serves another purpose, and Ben Folds tells us what in his lyrics: to keep our feet on the ground. Too much of philosophy has become a bunch of high-minded ideas which don't really relate to how we live our lives – that's why a lot of people consider the study of philosophy to be obscure and irrelevant (arguably, it can be). In considering the big existential weird and wonderfulness of life the high-minded philosophies are marvellous expressions of a rare art form and can even be fun. But. For living our daily lives we need to strip things back down to simply working out why we do what we do and then doing it the best that we can.

Taoism has its share of obscure pontification but there's a lot there that's pretty practical once you've lived with it for a while. I'm pretty sure, if you look long enough or have a bit of guidance from someone who knows the field, most philosophical, religious and spiritual approaches will have some very practical advice to offer.

In terms of developing your *Way* there will be some philosophical ideals that will be determined by the activity. The philosophy of Accounting, for instance, may include precision as a key ideal (note, it's an ideal to strive for, not something to beat yourself up for if you don't achieve it). The *Way* of Cake Baking, however, may have no place for precision. It may be primarily focused on intuition and allowing for 'wonderful accidents.'

Whatever your chosen path there may be an existing tradition that you can draw on. It could be the aesthetic of an artistic movement, or the philosophy of a martial art, it could be that the group of enthusiasts who pursue a particular activity already have a philosophical attitude that is an unspoken 'rule of the road.' It's for you to tease these things out. Some examples might be:

- Minimalism (an aesthetic)
- Stoicism (a Western philosophy)
- Wabi Sabi (a Japanese aesthetic)

- Servant Leadership (a management philosophy)
- Taoism (an Eastern spirituality and philosophy)
- Appreciative Inquiry (an approach to organisational change)
- Zen (an Eastern approach to Buddhism which has been widely adopted in the West)
- Aristotlean (philosophy in the tradition of Aristotle)
- Pragmaticism (a Western philosophy)
- Dadaism (a Western aesthetic)
- Judo (a Japanese empty hand martial art)
- Renaissance (a period in European history with a distinct flavour and outlook)
- Surfing (it has a distinct philosophy amongst it's serious practitioners and you stand out if you don't know it)
- Six Sigma (an approach to organisational efficiency and effectiveness)
- Humanistic (an approach to psychotherapy, counselling, teaching and care)

As you can see from this list (which is just a tiny selection) there are a massive range of philosophical outlooks (whether that's what they call themselves, it's what I'm calling them). They are all essentially about having a defined and considered approach to a particular field of human endeavour.

In my personal pursuit of 'The *Way* of throwing playing cards like a ninja,' I have developed my own philosophy for the practice. I have been able to draw heavily on Kyudo (the Japanese martial art of archery).

Kyudo talks a lot about the archer being 'one' with the bow, the target, and the arrow, so that they do not so much 'shoot' the arrow, as the arrow fulfils its purpose as a natural extension of the moment. This is part of how I approach throwing cards (and yes I do know that sounds a little silly, and that's part of why I enjoy it!). Other qualities which I invest in and develop when throwing cards are:

- being centred and relaxed (the fact is, if you're not, the cards don't fly)
- feeling peaceful while active
- and combining a sense of spiritual focus while maintaining a sense of humour (I am, after all, throwing playing cards across the room!).

You can see there that some of the philosophy is dictated naturally by the activity (i.e. the cards won't fly if I'm not relaxed); while other things are in there because they are qualities I want to develop – things I want to teach myself - through my practice of the art or *Way* (i.e. feeling peaceful while active).

Whether there is an existing Way you want to draw examples from or not, I have 3 suggestions for qualities which I have found to exist in one form or another in many Ways. I think they exist in many domains because they are positive qualities for us to endeavour to promote in ourselves as human beings, and because they help to make the practice a richer environment. For both of these reasons I offer these qualities to you as possible candidates for your Way as you develop it. The qualities are:

- Presence

- Non-attachment

- Respect

Presence is about constantly trying to be 'in the moment' in what you are doing. Have you ever been doing something (or even *Do*-ing something!) and really trying to do it well but you can't get you brain to shut up? Maybe you had an argument earlier in the day and you keep working it over in your head, maybe you keep getting that feeling like you forgot something, or maybe you want so much to be good at what you're doing it's like there's a constant commentator in your head (and some days they say nice things, other days, not so nice, right?). Any of these streams of thought - whether the voices are whispering success in your ear or predicting failure – any of them can be distracting in crucial moments when your mind needs to be fully immersed in what you are actually **doing** in that moment.

On the flip side, have you ever had an experience of being 'in the zone?' Your mind just goes quiet and all there is, is you, the thing you're doing, and an intuitive feeling for what you're doing right here, right now. Well, that's Presence, and here's the good news: Presence can be learnt. Like anything else, it just takes practice. The best way to practice it is to pursue a *Way*. By having this activity you do basically the same way over and over again, you have an environment where you can experience everything from excitement to frustration, to boredom, to tiredness – the whole run of your internal life – and train yourself to stay Present whatever is going on. So your *Way* is enriched by being present when you're practising it, and you get more able to be Present by practising you *Way*. Cool huh?

Non-attachment is a phrase most commonly seen in Buddhism, but I think it's pretty darned useful in every aspect of life. Basically you can choose to be attached to something, or detached from it, Non-attachment is the third option. Get it...? Well here's another way to get a hold of the idea:

Pick up your keys (or another object that's not breakable). Hold them in your closed fist with your palm facing down towards the floor. Now you're attached to them.

OK? You got that one?

Right, now open your fist. If my instructions are good enough, your keys (or whatever) have just fallen on the floor. Now you're detached from them.

Making sense so far?

Final one, pick your keys back up and have them sit on your open palm, palm facing upwards. They are in your hand, but someone could come and pick them up from your palm. Now you're Non-attached to them (physically anyway – you're probably pretty emotionally attached to them, that's a whole other journey)

Hopefully that little experiment has helped you get a hang of the idea of Non-attachment. It's a much bigger deal to be genuinely Non-attached to everything in your life (some might consider that the next best thing to enlightenment), but in terms of how all this applies to developing your *Way*, it's about Non-attachment to results. When practising throwing playing cards like a ninja, if I am too focused on getting them flying a certain way all the time then I'm going to get frustrated when they don't fly that way. By letting go of fixed ideas about how I want things to turn out (in terms of the result) I can enjoy the basic experience of throwing the cards a lot more. My frustration doesn't get in the way and it's easier to keep my mind clear and focused on the throw. You may be realising that Non-attachment to results will also help me be more Present. I will be able to just be in the moment of what I am doing rather than my mind racing ahead a few moments or even hours to try and conjure up how things will work out (such projection into the future in my mind can go a long way, even years – imagine how cool it would be if I got so I good I could become a world famous card thrower like Ricky Jay... pretty distracting...). All this doesn't mean that there isn't some kind of outcome that I am aiming for, it just means I'm not attached to it turning out like that. Sometimes the best things happen by accident!

I've talked about Presence and Non-attachment, now how about the last one: Respect. I expect you know a fair bit about this already but I'll say a few words... I want to mention two sides of Respect – respect for yourself and respect for others. In the context of pursuing your *Way*, respect for self is about how you approach the practice. Do you make choices about how, when and where to practice that take care of the potential vulnerability which comes with trying to be the best version of yourself that you can? When you have a bad day and don't manage to fit your practice in how do you bring yourself back to the task? Many of us (and it has been a long journey for me to unlearn this pattern) internally beat ourselves over the head with an imaginary stick called 'Discipline.' It's a painful and essentially self abusive method of motivating ourselves to action and often ultimately damaging to the practice long term. Sure, short term it might get you out of bed, up and moving right now but eventually the practice you have lovingly crafted into a *Way* is so completely associated with the ritual self-flagellation that the joy has, frankly, been beaten out of it.

On the flip side if I always let myself off the hook completely then my practice is likely to be very patchy. So how do we keep up our practice and still Respect ourselves? I've heard this description from a few people teaching meditation over the years: the mind is like a fairly dim dog. If when the dog wanders off you drag him back, beating him all the way he will just learn to be aggressive and may eventually run away completely. If however, when the dog wanders off (as he will, God bless him), you can just compassionately guide him back to where you want him again, and again, and again –

eventually he'll learn a new habit. Know now: it is highly likely you will have patches where it is difficult to keep motivated in your practice. All you need to do is compassionately, but firmly, lead your mind back to the task over and over again. Too little discipline or too much and you're probably not respecting yourself.

There are many ways that a lack of self respect can surface within a practice, the important thing is to be vigilant, and keep the intention to continually invoke a sense of respect in all that you do. I've done my best to point out one or two of the common pitfalls, to try and cover all the ways we manage not to respect ourselves could probably be a book all of it's own. Now it's up to you to be aware in your practice, and creative in how you tackle the tough stuff.

So, what about respecting others? If your *Way* is one which involves other people then hopefully this is pretty obvious. For instance, the *Way* of Football can be pursued in a 'win at all costs' kind of way, but you are likely to lose friends that way and eventually end up playing on your own because no-one wants to go home with another injury. How different would our sports be if we brought the Samurai attitude to the pitch? The Samurai wanted to be at their best in battle, not out of an ego-driven desire to win, but out of total respect for their opponents. If I am not at my best then even if you win, it will be a hollow victory for you. What if our sense of competition changed from 'I'm going to beat you' (even the language of it is aggressive) to 'out of a sense of service and respect, I want to give you the best challenge that I can.' In competitive environments, this is the potential shift that can happen when we really focus on Respect for others.

In terms of solo practices, like cake baking or writing, Respect for others can still be as important as Respect for self when it comes to the philosophy. It could again contain a sense of service to others, or relate to the content of what you produce. However, it can be much more subtle than that. How do you respect your partner, children or house-mates in when you choose to practice or how you choose to practice? If part of the way you practice the *Way* of Cake Baking involves having music playing, it may be best not to practice at 3am. If part of your approach to the *Way* of Writing involves using an old-fashioned mechanical typewriter it would be considerate and respectful to do it in another room when your husband is trying to watch TV. Sure that's your favourite chair for writing in but what about the philosophy of your practice?

This highlights one of the really valuable things about having a philosophy – it can keep you to the spirit of your *Way* without you getting rigid about the details. Presence, Non-attachment, and Respect (self and others). These are my suggestions for basic building blocks of a philosophy for your *Way*. Take 'em or leave 'em, it's up to you, they really are just suggestions and even if you take them up you may want to find your own words for them. I will also say that you don't have to write your whole philosophy down. It can be helpful to define it that way but many *Ways* out there have unwritten rules. For that matter, *Bushido* – the *Way* of the Samurai existed from around the 1200's but was not written down until the early 1900's and even then this was to help outsiders to understand it. Even in the very elegant writing that tried to define it, I'm sure a lot was lost in terms of the true depth and subtle beauty. I'd say, don't be afraid to write some stuff down to help you better understand it even if it's not quite perfect; but embrace the bits that you know in your heart but can't pin down for others. Those mysterious bits can be the richest aspects of any *Way*.

Next, I've offered some useful questions to ask yourself while developing the philosophy of your *Way*. As I mentioned before it can help to get someone else to 'interview' you and help you tease out the beautiful details and find the right words and phrases. If you are working with an interviewer then it might help to refer back to the guidelines I wrote on page 17.

Question set 2: Finding your Philosophy

a) What qualities do you most admire in others?

b) What do you want there to be more of in the world? How can you contribute to there being more of this/these things by how you are as a person?

c) What are the essential, life giving qualities of the activity (your chosen Way) when performed at it's best?

d) Imagine yourself in a years' time. Got it? What kind of person would you like to be? What would you like to be known for (qualities, not achievements).

e) How about 3 years time?

f) How about 5 years?

g) Why are you doing what you're doing? (you may not know the answer now, but keep asking yourself the question.)

Form

Chapter 4: Form

So, once you've chosen the activity you will develop into a *Way* (or *Do*) and started to define the philosophy of this practice (the qualities you wish to develop by engaging in this *Way*), the next step is to define the form the practice takes. You might think "well, if I'm practising the art of cake baking then I know what the form is: baking cakes." In a sense, you'd be right, but to just bake cakes is not the *Way*, it is not the *Do*, it is just an everyday activity. To make it a *Way*, you have to heighten the activity so that it calls for a greater state of presence, and a sharpened sense of awareness. This is what differentiates *Do*-ing something from just doing something, and what creates the *Way* as a path through which we can blossom. Defining the philosophy is the first step towards this. By defining the philosophy you clearly lay out the underlying purpose of the activity you are engaging in. The surface purpose might be baking a cake, but the underlying purpose is to cultivate in yourself those qualities you have set as the philosophy of the art. Get it?

So, the Form is the very particular way you do this activity when you are practising. If we take the *Way* of Cake Baking as an example: If you were just baking a cake you'd go into the kitchen, look at the recipe and get on with baking the cake, right? If you are engaging in the *Way* of Cake Baking then even before you enter the kitchen you need to have established a particular mind-set. Here is an example of what this *Way* might look like:

Pause outside the kitchen door and take a deep breath. Enter the kitchen and mindfully put away anything that is not needed. Wipe down the surfaces and lovingly wash your hands – not just to clean them but to prepare for what you are about to do. Set the recipe up in the right place so you can easily see it. Take out all the ingredients you are going to need and arrange them in the order you will need them. Take out your favourite mixing bowl and wooden spoon; pause, close your eyes and take a deep breath, on the out breath open your eyes and tap the edge of the mixing bowl with the spoon 3 times for luck....

I could go on, but hopefully you get the idea. When we are engaging in a practice in this manner, when we are developing our *Way*, every action is significant and has the potential to add to or take away from the experience, and how we blossom through it. The philosophy will help to determine how you do things. In the example above I've said "lovingly wash your hands..." but depending on the philosophy you are bringing to the practice it could be that washing hands is starkly functional, has several stages, or is the moment that allows you to focus your mind on what you are about to do. What I hope you are beginning to see is that by ritualising a thing, by giving it prescribed steps which we repeat over time, the activity becomes richer and deeper as an experience. A daily activity can become an oasis of soulful connection through which we learn about ourselves and nourish that part of us that craves meaning and significance. The three taps of the spoon on the side of a bowl which in everyday life we might dismiss as childish and superstitious is safely contained in a special activity. It serves to engage our imagination and bring present a quality which we desire to evoke through the activity. Really what we are doing here is taking an everyday activity and making it a special activity. Any activity can be special if we choose to bring that mind-set to it, and equally any activity can become mindless and dull if that is what we choose. Prayer can be a direct communion with our creator, or an irritating waste of time; sex can be a delicious connection with a lover or a mechanical satisfaction of a basic urge – your choice.

So: How do we make an activity special? How do you create your form?

Ritual
Now when I say ritual I don't mean something religious or dancing naked and slaughtering a chicken, I just mean a defined pattern of behaviour that frames the practice. It is this framing of the practice that sets it apart and makes it special. The simplest version of a ritual has something to denote a beginning, some stuff that happens in the middle, then something to denote an ending. There may be aspects of the middle bit that are defined as being a certain way – and I'd say there being regular touch points of structure will help you remain present. As a beginner to

a practice (and even as a veteran), generally speaking the more freedom you have, the easier it is to drift off and stop paying attention. However the middle doesn't need to be structured: it is the frame of beginning and ending that creates the container for something special to happen, some 'time out of time.'

An example where the middle isn't structured:

Throwing playing cards

I start off by walking around the room I'm using and clearing it up a bit. This is practical in that it will make it easier to find the cards after I have thrown them, but also I use it as a metaphorical practice where just as I clear the outer space I clear space in my mind too. I breathe deeply and try and get to as relaxed a place in myself as possible, emptying my mind of thoughts. When I feel ready and I've worked out where I'm going to stand to throw the cards I get the deck of cards, take them out of the box, place the box out of the way and then pause. I pause to centre myself and relax my body, then I begin throwing cards. At various intervals if I can see the cards aren't flying well, I'll pause to relax again. I collect up the cards when I run out and then throw again, but generally speaking the practice is pretty relaxed and 'formless.' Sometimes I set up some targets to throw at, sometimes I just throw at the wall. When I'm done, I more slowly and carefully collect up the cards, setting them all the right way up in a stack, with a similar feeling to at the beginning, whereby I am clearing the space and clearing my mind at the same time. I put the cards back in the box, then back on the shelf, and try and put the room back how it was only perhaps a little better, or a little tidier.

Hopefully you can see there a clear beginning, a less defined middle, then a clear end. The philosophy is expressed with it being primarily about being centred and relaxed, non-attached to results while striving for improvement, enjoying the fun and sensation of getting cards to fly through the air, and leaving myself and the world around me a little better than when I started.

Here is an example where the middle is structured:

Karate

I find a place to practice that feels right. I stand, feet together, hands by my side, centre myself, then bow. I bring my hands up to the start position, then begin the kata (kata is Japanese for form). Every movement is prescribed in significant detail, when to take a breath, the intention behind the movement, what I am imagining – everything follows a pattern taught to me by my teacher. I have repeated this pattern many times, and many people have done so before me over many years. When I complete the final movement of the kata, I step back so that my feet are together, my hands by my side, and bow.

Again, beginning and ending are clearly defined (bow in, bow out), and in this example, the whole of the content is too (every movement is prescribed). All of it defined and

enriched by the philosophy which underpins the practice:
Respect (the bow is representative of respect, and the kata
begins and ends with this), mindfulness, presence, natural
strength, relaxation with power, minimum effort for
maximum effect, no extraneous movement, investing the
practice with your whole being... and many other things.
Karate is an ancient practice with a very rich background
of philosophy which is passed on by the best teachers as
an integral part of the physical practice.

So you can see, both of the above examples and
many other things we do in life are ritualised. For a more
regular example think of theatre – everyone agrees to
come together at a certain time in a special room and all
be quiet while a story is told in an unusual way, and when
it's done everyone knows to clap to show their
appreciation, then we go home and talk about what we
liked and didn't like. Theatre is a ritual. So are office
meetings: people go at a certain time, sit around a table,
someone leads the meeting and we call them the 'Chair' -
see, it even has ritual language?! There is an agenda and
when the agenda is done there will probably be 'any other
business.' When the meeting is finished we leave and no-
one is surprised when they get sent 'minutes' of the
meeting. It's a ritual. So rituals are not unfamiliar
territory for us, it's just unusual for many of us to think of
things that way. In developing your *Way*, it will be useful
to spot the rituals in your life and make choices about the
rituals you want to keep repeating and the ones you want
to let go of. In terms of developing a practice, creating a
ritual framework for it will help you to engage the right

mindset for the activity you want to practice.

So, if ritual is the method for setting your activity apart from everyday life to help make it your *Way*, how can we make that *Way*, that practice as rich, engaging and nourishing as it possibly can be? It needs to engage us on all levels. Now, there are lots of ways of defining what the many levels of our being are and smarter men and women than me have made it central to their life's work to define different aspects of human being-ness, but I'm going to keep it pretty simple and if you want to get more elaborate as you develop your practice, your *Way*, then that's just fine and entirely up to you.

I'd say there are 4 key parts of yourself you need to make sure are stimulated by and invested in your practice:

- Body
- Emotions
- Attention
- Imagination

Now I realise that you may have been expecting spirit and mind to be in there, but those are both abstract concepts. What is the mind really? Your brain? Your ideas? Your self concept? No. That is far too messy a conversation to be getting into now: we want to be practical. As for spirit, let's not even start that one – some people would argue it doesn't even exist – best left to another conversation. Body and emotions are both reasonably easy to define (though not necessarily control!); Attention is just that – that you have your attention engaged with what you are doing (we all know what someone means when they say "pay attention"). Imagination is that faculty with which we create pictures in our heads, dream about the future, and conjure new ideas into being. Arguably attention and imagination could both be attributed to the mind, and yet are also intimately connected with the world of spirit, and spiritual practice (how would we create an image of God or the universe without an imagination, and how on Earth would we practice meditation or pray without engaging our full attention?). So, those are the four key aspects that I think you need involved to have a rich and nourishing practice. Now let's look at what it means to really involve these parts of ourselves...

Body

To really fully involve your body in a practice may seem obvious in some practices – like tennis – or seem much less obvious in other practices – like writing. However, in my opinion it is exactly the tension between the body's involvement in such outwardly different practices that can point us towards how we can engage our bodies in any practice, in any Way. As human beings we are embodied beings. There is nothing that we do that does not involve our bodies. While once psychology suggested that the mind shapes the body, it is now widely recognised that the body equally shapes the mind. If we consider thinking purely as it occurs in the physical brain, it is enabled by connections between neurons. We begin with a bunch of neurons and not so many connections, and then as we learn things we build new connections. These connections are created by repeated action. When I first take a new action it creates a new connection between previously unconnected neurons. When I repeat that action it reinforces and enlarges that connection. Our mind is formed, developed and expanded through action. If I don't take new actions then I don't form new connections, and I am limited in having new thoughts.

As such my writing is limited or enabled by the range of my embodied experience, and I would argue that unless you are really consciously connected to your body as you write, then you will limit the possible range of your writing. If you are limited in your access to your body then you are equally limited in your access to new thought. How you sit or stand, your posture, your basic fitness, and how you love and own (or disown) your physical form will affect your every action whether it is obviously 'physical' or not. This doesn't mean that someone who is disabled will necessarily be more limited in creative thought than someone who is able-bodied. Many examples of brilliant thinkers who are physically disabled would refute that. Stephen Hawking is a prime example. It is a lack of <u>connection</u> with your body which I think will limit your range of thought and this can be supported or undermined by many factors.

This is true not just for the mind but for the emotions, the imagination and the attention:

- Your emotional state is affected by your bodied state – it's really hard to stay angry when you're physically relaxed - try it!

- Your imagination is also affected by your physical state. Have you ever noticed how much easier it is to be creative or daydream when you have been lying on the sofa for a little while? Or when you've gone for a walk and have that nicely-tired-relaxed feeling?
- Equally your attention is impacted by your physical state: have you ever tried concentrating on something when you have an insect bite that's really itching?

At its core, while I am going to talk about each of the 4 faculties I have mentioned separately, they are completely interdependent on each other. I am talking about them separately to help access the full range of experience and so that you can make sure all your aspects are conscious and integrated rather than unconsciously dragged along for the ride.

This kind of conscious integration is what is in danger of being missed out in more obviously physical endeavours. To take my earlier example of playing tennis, it would be easy to think of this practice and go 'well of course my body is involved, I'm playing Tennis! Duh!' and leave it at that. However, if you really want to plumb the depths of your practice and turn it into your *Way* then you will need to examine even the most obvious aspects of your art or craft. So with Tennis as the example of a fairly physical *Way*, how can you get the richest experience out of your body while playing? It's not even about being more physically skilled in it (although that may be part of it – pro's spend hours just on getting their footwork right). What about your physical sensation? How about your sensual enjoyment of your physical surroundings? The sun overhead, the breeze on your face, the grass underfoot... it's really about getting maximum awareness of yourself and your environment through your physical being while engaged in your *Way*. A *Way* is about the world, not just about you.

A great method to really connect with your body and yourself as a physical being is to work through your whole body top-to-toes or toes-to-top within your practice. You can do this at the start of each practice session or use it as a gradual deepening process within your *Way*: working with one part at a time and practising with awareness of that part for a few sessions or weeks before moving on to the next part. I personally like to start at the bottom, so here's a suggested list with examples for writing and tennis:

- Feet – how do your keep your feet on the ground while you write? What is your footwork like on the court? Are you stable? Heavy-footed or light-footed (if you're too heavy footed it is not to do with weight but ineffective movement habits and the shock of impact will echo up from your feet through the rest of your body – not great for your joints)?
- Ankles and lower legs – are your ankles loose and relaxed while you write? Your calves? Are your ankles fluid and relaxed when you move but well

supported by your calves?

- Knees – are your knees comfortable and soft when you're writing (it's easy for knees to get a bit forgotten and bent out of shape under the desk!)? Are your knees fluid and effective at helping you transition your weight when you move on the court? Are you being careful not to twist in the knee joint when you change direction suddenly (footwork practice again helps with this)?

- Thighs – are your thighs toned but not tense when you sit, supporting your legs or do they flop outwards (this can put more pressure on the knees)? Are your thighs active and engaged on the court to help your knees stay loose (be aware of if your knees fall inwards when you stand – this is often because the thighs have some 'lazy habits')?

- Pelvis – is your pelvis tilting forwards or back when you sit where you sit to write, or nicely balanced to support you spine? Is your pelvis engaged and toned but not tight when you move (if it's not engaged your upper and lower body won't really work together, but if it's too tense you'll lack grace, flow and power)?

- Spine – the spine is the centre of your whole body and nervous system. Is your spine stacked nicely like a pile of coins, balanced and poised (not 'ram-rod-straight')?

- Belly – is your belly and lower back relaxed allowing you to breathe deeply using your diaphragm?

- Rib-cage and Chest – is your chest open but not pushed forwards, allowing your rib-cage to expand in all directions when you breathe?
- Shoulders – are your shoulders relaxed but not 'dead' when you sit at your desk? Are your shoulders relaxed so your arms are supported and connected to your back and whole body when you swing the racket?
- Elbows and forearms – are your elbows and forearms engaged but not tense when you type or write? Are you careful not to overly 'snap' the elbow joint or over-tense it and the forearm on impact with the ball?
- Wrists and hands – do you take your hands off the keyboard or page and move and flex them differently as part of your writing practice (this helps them not to get too 'stuck' and tense, and keep good blood-flow going through them)? Is your grip 'alive' on the racket handle so that you can really carefully control the racket through the subtleties of your grip? Are the muscles around your wrist toned and alive enough without being tense so that you don't damage the joint on those big hits?
- Neck and head – is your neck loose but supportive so your head can balance perfectly on top of your spine?
- Senses – When you write or play tennis: what can you see? What can you hear? What can you smell? What taste is in your mouth? What do you feel

against your skin?

The above is not an exhaustive list and I have grouped some parts of the body together. You could break things down a lot further, or take a less structured (but none-the-less thorough) 'scan' through your body from toes to head. Hopefully it gives you a flavour of how aware of your body it is possible to be in any activity – whether outwardly 'physical' or not.

Emotions

How you involve your emotions in your practice – your Way is also vital to consider. There is the basic level of bringing your emotions into the field of your practice through awareness. Just asking yourself how you are feeling before you begin your practice and afterwards could have a powerful effect on both your emotional awareness and on the quality of your practice. However, there is a step further. Once you are more aware of what is going on in the often murky and ephemeral realms of your emotions, you have the possibility to shape your emotions and to make positive use of them. This is closely connected with how vividly you can engage with your imagination (which we will deal with shortly) but to stick with emotions for now, whatever your Way, there will be an emotional state which is most conducive to effectiveness in your practice. Why not work to engender that emotional state whenever you practice? It is not about forcing yourself or repressing whatever emotion is there, it is about creating a positive emotional habit. If you work with emotionally 'checking in' before and after you practice, you may find that this kind of emotional shift is happening whether you intend it to or not.

Just as you can connect your practice, your *Way* with particular emotional states, you can also use your practice as an environment to explore whatever emotions you have going on in that moment. The *Way* is after all a way of life, not merely a hobby or pastime. You may well want to practice when you are feeling all sorts of things. I know for myself that grief, for instance, is an unpredictable feeling and can stick around for extended periods of time. Bringing these feelings to your *Way* can help you to learn how to have your feelings – whatever they are – and still go on living. I know that has been the case for me. I have trained Karate when I have been happy, sad, angry, grieving, in panic, excited, frustrated, joyous, scared, and many other things. Through it all the Karate practice has been a wonderful constant – never changing – and also an amazing ground for learning. By just allowing these feelings to be - while I practice – I have always learned something about that feeling. Sometimes – as it was with grief – it was just that life goes on, and while the feeling might not go away any time soon, neither would it destroy me. Sometimes it was that the feeling would go away sooner than I thought. Sometimes when I started my practice I knew I had a particular feeling going on but I wasn't sure why. Through the gentle osmosis of my practice, by the time I was done I knew why I was feeling what I was feeling and could do something about it. Sometimes – with Joy – it helped me to ground that feeling so I could really enjoy it.

A final way I'm going to suggest you can connect your emotions with your practice is by using them as 'fuel'. Boxing can be awesome when you're angry. Writing can be beautific when you're filled with melancholy. Perhaps accounting can help to tease the detail out of a sense of pure joy, making it all the more satisfying. Whatever the emotion and whatever your practice, connect them and see where it leads you. You can guarantee it will lead you deeper into your Way.

The key point in all of this is to consciously involve your emotions in your Way: they're going to be present anyway so you're better off inviting them in and making friends with them!

Attention

Most of us know what someone means when they say "pay attention," but not many people have really studied the quality of attention they bring to their endeavours. Is it sharp? Diffuse? Concentrated or dreamy? Out of duty or out of love? Do you pin your subject down with your attention or do you hold it gently within the field of your attention? In terms of your Way, I'd recommend getting really aware of the quality of attention that you are bringing to your practice – and indeed your life. It may be that your practice helps to engender a particular quality of attention, especially if this is part of it's philosophy and you have built the practice to reflect this. However, it is also going to be the case that sometimes your quality of attention will not be best suited to your practice – and may even be out of alignment with your philosophy. For instance, if you have been working on a detailed proposal for hours, your quality of attention is going to be sharp and focused like a razor. If you are then trying to practice the Japanese tea ceremony which requires your quality of attention to be light and diffuse like a cool breeze then it will be a tough transition. Equally if you are worried about something then you may be a bit distracted or lack focus. That is O.K, you're human, but with awareness you can ensure that your practice is not polluted and spoiled by a lack of attention or a discordant quality of attention. So much of what is required to elevate an everyday activity into a *Way* is awareness, and one of the great gifts of practising a *Way* is how it gives you a framework for cultivating greater awareness in your life.

Attention is such a refined thing to be aware of and as I've said before of other faculties, it is interconnected with all things. In you specifically: your body, emotions and imagination are all deeply affected by the quality of your attention. The imagination for instance is generally encouraged to operate by a diffuse attention. Emotions are best explored with direct attention but it needs to be a light touch, not aggressively chasing them. I tend to find that under this kind of light, direct attention my emotions gradually unfold and I find all the layers of emotion that sit underneath. Relationships tend to flourish when I bring a kind of warm loving attention, and I feel this physically as a kind of softening and opening in my chest – which could be described as an opening of my heart. I find I can chase physical aches and pains down in my body and this kind of 'hunting' quality of attention helps me find just the right spot to massage to relieve the pain.

What I am hopefully getting across is that just 'paying attention' is not enough. You need to get clear about what *kind* of attention is best suited to your *Way*, and there may be more than one depending on the complexity of your practice. With this raising of awareness about your quality of attention, I would hope you will also start to find this useful in the rest of your life – so this becomes a matter not only of how you practice your philosophy in your Art, but also how you live your philosophy in your life. For me, a *Way* is both a limited practice and my entire path through life. It is the microcosm and the macrocosm. As such, my practice should provide an environment filled with metaphorical significance where I can examine my actions, their consequences, and my subsequent actions and reflect upon what I can learn from the whole process. My insights in this environment should not just inform my future practice of the Art, but should also inform my understanding of how I am living my life. Thereby helping me to make more conscious choices about how I do that. Equally, I may learn things from other people or generally out-and-about in the world and it is vital that I bring these insights back to my Art to practice, test, and refine them. Microcosm feeds macrocosm feeds microcosm...and so on. This too is about attention. What quality of attention are you bringing to your life overall? Do you bumble along pretending you don't know what's happening? Do you steam-roller through life like you know what's what and no-one can tell you any different? Do you bring a noisy, acquisitive kind of attention to the world or a quiet and respectful one? Are you knowing or curious, or both? Are you loving or resentful?

If you imagine your life as a lover, how do you want to step out to meet it?

Imagination

The imagination is a muscle and for most of us who have gone through the Western education system, it is a sorely underdeveloped one. I really became aware of this when I trained as an actor and we had a tutor who would get us doing 'imagination work' for about three-quarters of an hour twice a day, every day. This was basically a kind of focused day-dreaming. It was focused in-so-much as it was from the perspective of the character we were developing in our rehearsals of a piece of theatre, but as long as we were working to step into their imaginal shoes we were encouraged to allow ourselves to follow whatever came up whether it was linear or not, whether we immediately understood it or not. This was raw exercise of the imagination and I don't think I'd ever done anything like it. Even day-dreaming happens by accident and is usually in an environment where something else is 'supposed' to be happening. This was an entire room full of people really bringing their attention to the practice of exercising and expanding their capacity for raw imagination.

You may or may not want to explore your

imagination in this way yourself, but for your practice, your *Way*, and - I'd hazard - your life to be as rich as it can possibly be, you will need to engage your imagination in the process. For your practice and your *Way*, that will depend a bit on the nature of what you are doing. For instance, in physical practices whether they be sports or martial arts, it has been found that imagining what you will do before you do it can significantly improve performance. Also, if you are training moves that you will use later, investing them with intense imaginal impressions can add power and focus. An example my friend and Karate teacher Tom Maxwell gives: in martial arts if you are training a front kick, you could imagine that when you do it you are kicking down a door of a burning building to rescue a child. Just think how much more committed and therefore powerful your kick will be if you really embed that imagined image within your technique. These methods, as you may have already spotted, will also then help to engage your emotions positively in the activity as well. This adds to your effectiveness and from the point of view of developing a *Way*, immerses you more fully in the activity at hand.

Within more purely creative activities you may want to add in time to exercise the imagination rawly as part of your practice, but there are other applications as well. For instance, if you are baking cakes (or sculpting, or wood-carving, or making furniture etc. etc.) you could go into your imagination before you start, see the cake before you (or whatever you are making) and ask it how it wants to be or if it has any advice for you before you start. You might be surprised by what you learn! At the very least you move from having mastery over your media to relationship with your media – from control to collaboration. It's a profound shift that will have a ripple effect across your entire life.

As with your emotions, your imagination is going to be involved in the process of your practice, your life and your Way whether you like it or not. We are imagining things all the time – whether desired futures or feared catastrophic outcomes – wouldn't you like to make your imagination your friend rather than your enemy? Like a small child, if you leave them alone in the corner and don't have a relationship with them, is it any wonder that eventually they make mischief?!

On a larger, existential level, I would ask the question: if you can't imagine it, can you experience it? People manage to ignore, suppress or block out experiences all the time, and while I have definitely seen things I don't think I could have imagined specifically, I think it is the breadth of range of my imagination which gives me the capacity to be aware of all that I am. So, if you love life enough to want to see more of it, don't just travel around the world hoping to see more and more stuff (although that might help broaden your horizons), take your imagination out for a run once in a while! Then when you do travel, you'll really see a lot more of what the world has to offer.

A note about Intention
Intention is a vital factor in any endeavour. What is your

intention in pursuing your *Way*? This is the application of the word intention as something you possess, a singular thing attached to a specific action or pursuit. There is also intention as a faculty, like attention or imagination. Lots of people define it different ways, I see it as a combination of attention and imagination (hence why this is a note!). I can pay attention to something without there being any thought of how I want it to turn out, attention is not directional or desiring by it's nature. Intention has direction. I attend to light a fire, I intend for it to get bigger. My attention is on the TV, my intention is to learn from it (as opposed to passively letting it wash over me). My attention is on that seagull over there, my intention might be to: watch it, study it, catch it, kill it, eat it, stroke it, love it, follow it... you see what I mean? Attention and intention are different. Intention has direction. And... I would say that our capacity to create that direction comes from our imagination. I can't intend any of the above things towards the seagull if I can't first imagine them to be possible. I may want to have solid knowledge or experience that a seagull is edible in order to intend to eat it, but if I was hungry enough then I might see it walking around, get a picture in my head of stuffing it in my mouth, and then intend to do just that! Equally, I can imagine eating the seagull but unless I bring some attention to achieving that task, it's just a picture in my head, not an intention.

I'm not saying I'm right and as soon as we start separating and defining things all sorts of opinions get involved. For what it's worth I think Intention as a faculty is the combination of imagination and attention. Whatever it is, I hope this little discourse has made you consider what kind of a thing Intention might be and off the back of that thinking, you'll look to make use of your intention in discovering, creating, practising and sustaining your *Way*.

The Interdependence of the whole

I know I have already stated this in the bit on the body and at various points along the way, but I think it bears saying again: all of these faculties are completely interdependent upon each other, any separation is an illusion! It's a useful illusion because it makes it easier to discuss these things but an illusion none-the-less. It is worth being really aware that when you focus on any one aspect, you cannot help but affect the others as well. Nothing exists in isolation. So... the overriding point here is: whatever you are doing, whatever you find or create your *Way* to be, make sure *all of you* is involved. The involvement of your whole being and the total engagement of yourself with the world around you is central to pursuing a *Way* (*Do*-ing stuff) rather than just doing stuff.

Now, go forth and build your Form for your practice, your *Way*. Ensure your Form and your Philosophy connect up and mutually support each other so that your Form is your philosophy embodied. You want to be living your *Way* not just have it as a nice idea.

"Knowledge is a rumour until it is lived in the muscle."[4]

Below I offer some useful questions to ask yourself while developing the Form of your *Way*. As mentioned before it can work really well to get someone else to 'interview' you and help you tease out the beautiful details and find the right structures and nuances of action. If you are working with an interviewer then it might help to refer back to the guidelines I wrote on page 17.

---

4   I've heard this at least 4 different places and I've no idea who said it first!

Question Set 3: Finding your Form

a) What things do you need to do every time you practice?

b) Do any of these things connect with the philosophy you have laid out? If so it may be worth emphasising them within the practice so that your Way helps you embody your philosophy.

c) Is there anything that is not a necessary part of the activity but you would like to add in to help anchor an aspect of your philosophy in the practice?

d) Is there a special way you can begin your practice to set the tone?

e) Is there something you can do to end your practice so you feel complete at the end of a session?

f) How can you involve your Body in your practice?

g) How can you integrate your Emotions?

h) How can you ensure you fully bring your attention to your practice? (ritual, structure, and a clear beginning and end help!)

i) How can you involve your imagination in your practice?

Practice

Chapter 5: Practice

In the course of this book I have talked about practice a lot. Not always explicitly, and often in the context of 'a practice' (or set of practices), however, practice is central to what we are about here. My friend Clare Myatt[5] likes to say: "Practice makes permanent." I completely agree. Further to that, we are practising *something* all the time. Practice is just repeating something over and over again. If you are mindful of what you are doing then your practice will be more fruitful, but the repetition alone works. So, whatever you are doing now, is part of your practice. Whatever patterns you repeat in your life – whether you are happy about them or not – you are practising those patterns. This is true right down to how your brain is made up. As I touched on earlier, when you learn something new you make new connections in your brain, when you do that thing again, you strengthen those connections.

The primary question I'm going to offer you in this chapter is: **What do you want to practice?**
This is why it is so important to get clear about your philosophy first: you are deciding what you are practising, and in doing so you are essentially deciding *who you are going to be*. Not as a dream in your head but as who you are in your life. So, I'll ask you again: What do you want

---

5   www.claremyatt.co.uk

to practice? Really, that is the core question we have been working on for the whole of this book. Your greatest potential art work is your one unique and special life. Whatever you practice is your life, your art, your *Way*. At times I have been talking about the refined art of throwing playing cards like a ninja, or cake baking, or accountancy, and any of these things may seem inconsequential, or overly simple, or dull. That said, as far as I'm concerned any of these activities, indeed any activity we undertake in our lives is potentially a forum to refine ourselves at the deepest level of our beings and to fulfil our life purpose. If you can find something you enjoy and then find ways to be more conscious about how you do it then: (a) you will do it repeatedly because you enjoy it, and (b) by repeating it you will cement in yourself a way of being that is the very essence of why you are on this planet. In the moment of practising that activity and in all the subtle ways that it informs the rest of your life, anything – throwing playing cards, cake baking, accountancy, or any of a billion other things you could spend your time doing (or I should say *Do*-ing) – can support you in being more of who you really are and making the world a better place. I offer the quote from Howard Thurman again (because it's just so brilliant!):

"Don't ask yourself what the world needs; ask yourself what makes you come alive. And then go and do that. Because what the world needs is people who have come alive."

In my experience, finding the 'big picture,' whole life version of what makes you come alive can take some time and some work, but start small and build a practice out of what is available to you right now. Throw playing cards, bake a cake, play tennis, or crunch some numbers. By practising what is alive for you right now you set your feet on the path that may one day lead you to the big picture of Life Purpose. The Taoists talked of 'the virtue of the small.' I think this is what they were talking about: the small is the big only...smaller! You could spend your whole life practising something you think is small, always with one eye open for the big Life Purpose, and then get to the end of your life and realise: I have brought more light, and life, and joy to the world through my small actions than anything big I could have done. Maybe not, but unless you know exactly what the big thing is right now then what's the harm in joining me in an experiment and doing the small things with consciousness, and heart and commitment – at the least you'll have some fun and improve a skill.

So, that's why to practice, now let's look at how to practice...

The Practice Continuum

The practice continuum is a model I came up with a couple of years ago to help distinguish different attitudes we can have within any given activity. It's helpful in understanding how practising works so we can get conscious about not just what we're doing but how we're doing it. It might sound complicated when I describe it like that (especially with that fancy name I've given it huh?!), but it's a pretty simple concept once explained. Here it is, I'll explain it in a minute:

Practising   **Acting**   **Doing**

Each of these attitudes to action can be brought to any activity and reflect a range from taking action purely for the sake of the action itself and it's normal outcomes, through to taking that same action but with little concern for the outcomes and a strong focus on what you might learn while you take the action. I'll explain them one at a time:

Practising
This is when you are taking an action or engaged in an activity – lets say juggling – and while you are definitely wanting to succeed in that task (i.e. throwing and catching the balls) you are also focused on the process of what you are doing (i.e. how accurate your throws are, how elegant your catches are, if you add in any tricks, or walk around while juggling). So this is when you are engaged in an activity to...well... Practice! You are working to improve your skill in the activity, you are analysing how you are doing it rather than just doing it.

When 'Practising' you may even separate out sections of the activity and repeat them to refine a certain aspect of what you're doing. For instance, with Juggling, even if you are working on juggling three balls you might take some time to just toss one ball from hand to hand to improve your throwing and catching and to refine the arc of the ball. By doing this you are still practising for juggling three balls even though you are not actually engaged in the act of juggling three balls.

The key here is that 'Practising' is not just focused on doing the thing, it is about learning about and improving the doing of the thing.

When I practice my Karate I probably look like I don't know what I'm doing to an outside eye. I will stop in the middle of a movement or sequence and do it several times to see what it feels like to do it differently, I may laugh and stop when I mess something up, I am not invested in doing a perfect and smooth version of the form. That said, as part of the session I may do one run through to do it smoothly to practice 'doing it smoothly' but that is not what the whole session is focused on. If there are any patterns within the activity that I want to change, this is the forum to work for those changes. I will now contrast the opposite end of the spectrum.

Doing
This is just getting on and doing it! There is little or no analysis here and I am fully invested in 'getting it right'. If

I have any patterns I am not happy with in the activity I am not paying attention to that. I need to have done plenty of 'Practising' and then when I come to 'Doing' I can just be present, get in the zone and go for it. If I am doing a performance as a juggler then I need to just be focused on smiling and acting up to the crowd – I can't be thinking about the fact that when I throw with my left hand it goes a bit wonky! I will need to manage that pattern but I am not engaged in trying to change it or master a new throw – that is the stuff of 'Practising.' In performance I have to trust that all the time I have put in 'Practising' is enough, and throw myself into the raw moment of the performance. It's not generally fun to watch someone trying to learn a technique – we want to see them when they have mastered it and make it look effortless and exciting! Similarly in sports – tennis for instance, you need to take time 'Practising' to improve your backhand but when you are playing in a competition you just want to be focused on the game, the ball and your opponent. If you are too internally focused and still 'Practising' in your head you are going to be too wrapped up on the inside to see all that you need to see on the outside. That's what people often mean when they say "You're over-thinking it." If you're focus is pulled out of the present moment by anything then you will not be playing at your best. That is why 'Practice' is so important: you have to get good technique so ingrained that when it comes to 'Doing,' you just do it, and you do it right.

That's the two polar opposites, now let's look at the

ground in between...

Acting

This really is the full range in between the two poles. I've put it in the middle but it could be anywhere along the spectrum – you could be Acting with a focus on Practising or Acting with a focus on Doing. I've called it Acting deliberately. That might seem like an obvious thing to say (I'm writing this book, of course I did it deliberately – Duh!) but what I mean is that I have chosen that word because of its other meanings. Acting because you are taking Act-ion, i.e. you are doing something; but also Acting because I think it is similar to the art of acting that takes place on a stage. Let me explain...

In theatre you have rehearsals (at the Practising end of the spectrum) and you have performances (at the Doing end of the spectrum). However, in both situations you have to really finely balance the Doing of the thing with the self-awareness of Practice. When you're rehearsing you can try out different ideas and stop and repeat stuff but there is also an inherent desire to have a flow to the scene or play that you're working on. What really is Practising in the terms that we are talking about it here is the stuff you do on your own – learning lines, rehearsing movements, imagining the world of the character, researching the time period, trying on the costume, etc. What happens in the rehearsal room has moved away from pure Practice and is on the continuum heading towards Doing. Equally when you are Performing, no matter how well practised and rehearsed you are, there is still some small bit of you that must remain extra aware of your environment and particularly the audience. It is a deep and subtle art which could take a whole book to itself, but to describe it at a gross level: if two people on stage are just having a conversation with each other then they would be turning their back to the audience and speaking quietly, or might even walk off the stage. What is going on is not just 'having a conversation'. They have enough awareness of the audience, themselves and the stage to keep their bodies open to the audience, to speak loudly enough to be heard, and to stay within the confines of the set. A great writer on the art of acting, Konstantin Stanislavski, described the creating and acting of a character as being like wearing a perfectly tailored coat but leaving the top button undone. It is this 'top button undone' that means acting really lives in the range between Practising and Doing. It is this fact that has lead me to call that whole middle area of the continuum 'Acting.' Hopefully, in describing my reasoning in this way I have also illustrated for you the range of experience that can sit between the two extremes.

Why are these distinctions important?
Whenever you are developing your *Way* or practising it (small 'p') you need to be aware of where you are on the continuum otherwise you don't know what you are doing. This might seem an extreme thing to say, after all if you're baking a cake you're baking a cake right? Well, yes and... you can be baking a cake to practise a new recipe, or try out a different balance of ingredients, or you can be

summoning the greatest refinement of your art, producing a cake you have Practised (big 'p') many times so that you can bake the best darned cake your friends have ever had! Surely, if you are practising the *Way* of Cake Baking having people enjoy the results has to be in the philosophy?! This is true of any activity you do. In any given activity there is the explicit outcome for that activity (i.e. making a cake, throwing playing cards, doing your accounts etc.) but there will be many other agendas at play as well. If you are not clear about these agendas you can end up trying 'Practising' but trying so hard to get it right that you never learn anything; or 'Doing' but constantly observing yourself on the inside thereby stopping yourself from finding any flow. To have a really developed *Way*, you need to get aware and specific about these agendas as much as is humanly possible. Your philosophy is an expression of the key agendas you want to fulfil. The quality of your practice is also core to why you are doing what you are doing and how you are doing it. So... Get aware of where you are on the practice continuum and be conscious in your decision to either work on embedding new skills and deepening existing ones, or forgetting the rules and just immersing yourself in the experience If you have Practised enough then even when you forget the rules, you will still embody the principles. Just as valid – as long as it is done with awareness – is being anywhere in between the two extremes. You could be looking to bake a really great cake but doing something experimental too. You could be throwing playing cards primarily for fun but still have a bit of an eye on how accurately you're throwing. See what I mean? The important thing, and the reason why this continuum is something I consider worth mentioning, is that this is another doorway to being ever more conscious and aware of what you are doing. It is a method to help you deepen your relationship with your *Way*. The more you know your *Way*, the more you know yourself. The more fully you can embrace your path (your *Way*), in my experience, the more fully you will be able to embrace life. As you refine your awareness through your practice, you open new ways of seeing yourself and the world.

"The real voyage of discovery consists not in seeking new landscapes, but in seeing with new eyes." --Marcel Proust

By seeking new landscapes we can actually help to keep ourselves blind. I touched on this idea in the section on developing your Imagination. The rush and excitement of a constantly changing environment is so stimulating that we never bother to look beyond the ends of our noses. Being with an unchanging vista will encourage you to look more deeply at the detail, richness and texture of what is there. I enjoy watching TV and films a lot but if I would offer one criticism of the media it is that programs and films are getting cut together so the images, shots and frames change faster and faster. The creators of these arts would say that it is a way to capture their audience's short attention span. I don't have any evidence to offer but I do wonder if this is a self-perpetuating cycle. Research says people have a short attention span, so film-makers film short shots and scenes, which encourages the attention span to be short so over time it shrinks and as the attention span shrinks the scenes and programs adjust to keep people's attention... and on until a soap opera is five minutes long total! I would suggest to you that it is a growth-ful and – once you get used to it – enjoyable thing to stretch yourself. Taking something and making it a deep and conscious practice is the best way I have found to really learn to 'see with new eyes' as Marcel Proust put it. To mindfully repeat a detailed process over and over for years gives you an apparently unchanging framework within which to realise that in the depth and repetition of the thing lies infinite detail and a source of real wonder.

There is a short Kata (pattern of movement) from Karate which I have been practising for over ten years and I am still learning new things about it and having new experiences. I'm not trying to tell you, you won't get bored sometimes, you probably will, but that is just a phase and one of the things that long term practice of a *Way* has taught me is how to live through the boredom. Life is going to be boring at times, it can be tough to live through but it's true. If the only solution you have is to run off and find a new experience then you'd better forget about marriage and children, and basically any long term relationships with people, places, jobs or things. Living through the tough times (and boredom can be one of the toughest things to live through and not give up) is a core life skill. Part of why I'm so passionate about all this '*Way* stuff' is that finding and practising your *Way* is hands-down the best method I've found for learning how to live a deep, long-term, satisfying life. As I've talked about before, your *Way* is a microcosm within which you can learn amazing lessons about the macrocosm of life. Now, I'm not saying it isn't fun and valuable to seek new experiences too – it is both of those things. I am trying to offer a window on why you'd create a ritual form for something you love doing and then repeat it regularly over the years. It'll always be the same routine, and... it'll never be the same again.

Special Time

It is important, particularly at the beginning, to set aside a bit of time on a regular basis to 'do some practice.' This is where the ritual Form of your *Way* will come into its own and you can fully immerse yourself in the activity. However, if this is all you do then you can end up with your practice being so separate from your life that it becomes cut off from it and far from making you more aware of your life it can be a distraction from really living your life. So you need to balance special time to practise with an integration of you *Way* into your life. Ideally your *Way* is your life and your life is an expression of your *Way*. This is where your philosophy comes into its own! If my philosophy for throwing playing cards for instance is to be relaxed, to have fun, and to not be too attached to the results, these are all things I can live by in anything I do. I can walk down the street embodying that. I can cook my dinner embodying that. I can phone my friend and listen to their problems and still embody this philosophy. Of course there may be some aspects of the philosophy that are very specific but most of it should be applicable in many areas of your life. This is how your Way becomes a way of life, not just a hobby. For that matter, the aspects of the philosophy that seem to be most specific to the activity you practice can be the juiciest ones to apply to the rest of your life. Just think, how can they be applied as metaphors? In this way the application of your Way and your philosophy to daily life can deepen your understanding of the practice in its specifics. The practise informs how you live life, and how you live life informs your practice.

All that said, how do you keep remembering to refer back to your philosophy moment-by-moment every day? Luckily, there is a wonderful old story that can help us with this! The story comes from Islam and is the story of why Muslims pray five times a day. I'll tell a version of it and if it is not wholly accurate then please accept my apology. In speaking of Islam I am a 'visitor in a foreign land' so-to-speak. I found this story really helpful when I heard it and I wish to share it.

One day Muhammed went to his cave on the mountain so he could ascend in spirit and speak with God. On his way through the layers of heaven he met Moses. They spoke briefly and Moses said to stop by on the way back to Earth. So Muhammed carried on and eventually came to the place where he would meet God. That day God decreed to Muhammed that his loyal followers should pray a thousand times a day so that they would remember their connection with God. Dutifully (if perhaps with some

71

trepidation) Muhammed said "Of course, we shall do as you say." On his way back to Earth Muhammed stopped off to see Moses and told him what had happened. Moses said "What? A thousand? You'll never get people to do that. Go back and ask God to make it less." Muhammed could see Moses' point and returned to God's presence to ask for a reduction. God – being both generous and infinitely forgiving said "Of course, let's half it, make it 500!" Muhammed was very grateful and relieved and headed back to Earth, stopping off to thank Moses for his suggestion on the way. "What?!" Cried Moses, "I thought you'd been a merchant? Don't you know how to bargain with someone? There's no way your followers will be able to pray 500 times a day no matter how devoted they are – when will they eat?! Go back and get a better deal." So Muhammed did as Moses said and went back to speak to God. Without any hesitation God agreed to reduce it "how about 100 prayers a day?" Muhammed was even more relieved and rushed off feeling very pleased with such a reasonable suggestion. He told Moses that on the way back to Earth... "Reasonable?! Listen Muhammed, I've led followers of God – and through some tough times, I'm telling you. It doesn't matter how devoted your guys are, they are not going to manage 100 a day." As you have probably guessed Muhammed ended up going back... several times more: 50, then 10, then 5. Even at 5 Moses suggested going back to God "Make it 1," he said "people can manage 1." But Muhammed stood firm: "I am too ashamed already at my bartering with God. I will not go any further. It will be 5." So he returned to Earth, went

*back down the mountain from his cave and taught his
people to pray 5 times a day to remember their connection
with their creator, and they still do to this day.*

If we apply this to the *Way*, of course it would be
ideal to remember and live our philosophy every moment
of every day, but if not every single moment, maybe a
thousand small moments. And if a thousand moments
feels like a lot to ask, maybe we can just start with five
and be working on it. However frequently you choose to
do it, you need some method to remind yourself to
connect with your *Way*. It might be that you set five
times a day and have an alarm on your watch, mobile
phone, or computer. It might be that you take a moment
every time you go to the toilet or make a cup of tea, or
walk through a door. You could put a dot of paint on
your watch face, or a sticker on your computer and every
time you notice it you pause and connect with your *Way*.
However you choose to trigger yourself to connect, this
kind of integration with everyday life is a vital companion
practice to your 'dedicated practice time' where you work
with your ritual Form.

You began by choosing an activity, then you defined your
Philosophy, then you created a Form for your *Way*, now
finally you have worked out how to fit it into your life –
both special practice time to work with your Form and
bringing your Philosophy into daily life so you have an
integrated practice. You are ready to live your *Way* and
you have created for yourself a *Way* of life. Pretty

awesome huh?!

I have some closing words to follow but I want to end this chapter on practice with the question I offered before and I encourage you to remember that anything you do repeatedly you are practising, whether you intended to or not. This is your one unique and special life:

What do you want to practice?

Closing words: Short book, long path...

This is a short book. That's deliberate. I wanted to offer you a framework to apply to your life and more specifically to something you love doing and wish to deepen your experience of. You'll probably get more skilful at it too but that's a by-product of the love and practice of it. I'm not giving you specifics on your art, your *Way*. As one of my teachers would say: "that's your fruit to pick."

One thing I do want to make clear though: just because it's a short book doesn't mean it's easy or quick to embody what is taught here. I would hope that would have become clear by now but I thought I'd better say it outright. If you choose to really commit yourself to a *Way*, it is a long path. That's sort of the point. A *Way* is a never-ending path – there is no goal, no gold at the end of the rainbow. The rainbow is just one of many beautiful sights you will see while walking the path – a landmark in your mind perhaps. A moment of remembrance. Give up goal-seeking or thinking that there's somewhere to get to. This is life. Don't hurry towards the end of it, just enjoy putting one foot in front of the other...

Appendices

Principles
and
Question Sets
(for easy reference)

Philosophy

Your *Way* needs to have a stated philosophy – a yardstick against which attitude, thought and action are measured

Form

Your *Way* needs to have ritual forms which clearly denote when you are engaged in practice. These signal to your psyche that something special is going on.

Practice

You have to practice your *Way*. That's how it works. If you are not doing it then the *Way* is just an idea, rather than a *Way*.

Question set 1: Finding your *Way*

a) What do you love doing? (don't count anything out, remember, I throw playing cards across the room).

b) You know that feeling you get where you are at your most alive, awake and alert – not from a rush of adrenalin but with a wholesome, satisfied deep breath and big smile kind of feeling? What are you doing when you feel like that?

c) Is there an activity which is difficult but you keep going back to it nonetheless because it's juicy, deepening and strangely satisfying?

d) What do you read up about, find websites about, study for and ponder even though it's not your job?

e) Is there an activity where you feel at home, like this is the thing you were born to do – that doesn't mean it's easy or that you're the best at it: It just feels right.

Question set 2: Finding your Philosophy

a) What qualities do you most admire in others?

b) What do you want there to be more of in the world? How can you contribute to there being more of this/these things by how you are as a person?

c) What are the essential, life giving qualities of the activity (your chosen Way) when performed at it's best?

d) Imagine yourself in a years' time. Got it? What kind of person would you like to be? What would you like to be known for (qualities, not achievements).

e) How about 3 years time?

f) How about 5 years?

g) Why are you doing what you're doing? (you may not know the answer now, but keep asking yourself the question.)

Question Set 3: Finding your Form

a) What things do you need to do every time you practice?

b) Do any of these things connect with the philosophy you have laid out? If so it may be worth emphasising them within the practice so that your Way helps you embody your philosophy.

c) Is there anything that is not a necessary part of the activity but you would like to add in to help anchor an aspect of your philosophy in the practice?

d) Is there a special way you can begin your practice to set the tone?

e) Is there something you can do to end your practice so you feel complete at the end of a session?

f) How can you involve your Body in your practice?

g) How can you integrate your Emotions?

h) How can you ensure you fully bring your attention to your practice? (ritual, structure, and a clear beginning and end help!)

i) How can you involve your imagination in your practice?

The Big question

Knowing that this is your one unique and special life:

What do you want to practice?

Guidelines for interviewing, and Forming a Group

If you're working together with someone else as an 'interviewer' (and I'd really recommend it – the conversations we have are the way we shape our world) then I offer here some guidelines for the interviewer:

1. It is your job to hear the story, not tell it – just listen.

2. If you hear something that intuitively makes your ears prick up: ask to hear more about it.

3. Take a few notes as you're listening. It will help you both to spot patterns, and where there's a pattern, there may be a Way.

4. Listen with an open heart – try not to judge what you hear, empathise with your partner in *Do*-ing.

5. Cultivate an attitude of fascination. One of my teachers, a wonderful lady called Jane Magruder-Watkins, has this great way of saying "Isn't that interesting..." She really means it and the way she says it makes you reconsider what you've just said and become fascinated in it yourself. That's what you're after (and don't give yourself a hard time if you don't quite get it, Jane's had a lot of practice).

Forming a Group

Doing things on your own is just fine. For some of us it suits us very well. However, it can also be unnecessarily lonely and make things much harder work than they need to be. Even the Buddha who spent hours, weeks, months, or even years essentially sat on his own said that the optimum conditions for achieving enlightenment meant having Sangha – which basically means a bunch of like-minded, like-hearted friends.

Now clearly, you may not find a whole group of people who all want to make accountancy their *Way*, or cake baking their *Way*, or throwing playing cards like a ninja their *Way*. You might, but you don't need to worry about it. Just the fact that you are practising a *Way* will give you common ground. To begin with you could get together with some friends to work through the Question Sets. Interview each other in pairs and share stories about what you are realising about the things you love, yourself and your life. Once you've established what you are each going to practice as a *Way*, keep meeting and sharing stories about how you are getting on. How are you integrating your practice into your life? What are you enjoying? What are you finding tough?

Then, every three or six months you could go through the Question Sets again. It may help you deepen your *Way* or gain new philosophical insights. It may just help you realise how far you've come.

Meeting like this also has an added bonus – you will be practising the *Way* of meeting as a group! This is something well worth practising, and if your experience is anything like mine then you may well find your friendships deepening, and not just with those you meet in your '*Way* group' but with everyone. Forming, nurturing and sustaining relationships is a skill in itself. Who you are is shaped by, even arguably defined by what you practice so if you want to be someone who shares community, asks for help when you need it, and supports your friends when they need it, then forming a '*Way* group' could give you the environment to practice those skills. Who knows, it could even become one of your favourite aspects of practising a *Way*.

Just like any other *Way*, meeting as a group is supported by having some kind of Philosophy and some kind of Form. This is what I have found: The Form is simple – find a mindful way to begin the session, a mindful way to end it, and have someone to keep time (especially if you are doing interviewing). For the Philosophy, you may want to work this out for yourself, but I will share some guidelines I learnt from my friend Rob Dreaming[6] who is a masterful holder of talk circles:

- Speak from the heart
- Listen from the heart
- Don't plan what you will say (you can't listen properly if you do)
- Be concise in what you say (so you don't hog the space)

_____

6 www.heart-source.com

Other resources, Acknowledgements, and Author Profile

Other Resources

Below I offer a few resources which I have found useful in exploring the *Way*...

The Tao Te Ching – I'm working on my own version but until then, the best translations I'd go for are by Gia-Fu Feng and Jane English; Ursula LeGuin; or Stephen Mitchell.

The Art of Practice – an audio program on CD by Lance Giroux available from his website www.alliedronin.com

Mastery – a book by George Leonard, grandfather of the Human Potential Movement.

The Tao of Pooh and the Te of Piglet – a very accessible book by Benjamin Hoff on Taoism.

Way of the Peaceful Warrior – a wonderful novel and now also a film. Book by Dan Millman.

There are many others I could list but they would all be aimed more at one specific *Way* rather than the broad area of finding **your** *Way*.

Acknowledgements

There are a great many people to whom I owe a debt of thanks for their assistance, challenge or support in finding and following my *Way* over the years and I am almost guaranteed to miss someone out so apologies up-front. Hopefully you all know who you are well enough, I'll do my best here.

My mum, Lyn and my dad, Fred – wonderful and supportive parents. My wife Miche and my new-born son Samson – Inspirations and beloveds. My numerous teachers over the years: Alan Chant, Syd Ralf, Judy Cowley, Steve Rowe, Anne Rowe, Niamh Dowling, Crazy Uncle Alex, Trish Baillie, Vic Cooke, Tom Maxwell, Andy Cundy, Simon Buxton, Howard Charing, Edmund To, Kate Shela, Shianna Ravenhill, Martin Nathanael, Kathryn Wallace, Nicola Coombe, Lizy and Ian Newton, Lance Giroux and many more. Companions on the path (definitely too many to mention) Jamie Morgan, Claire Breeze, Tom Anderson, Tessa Howell, Mark Walsh, Martin Saville, Clare Myatt, Pete Hamill, Deborah Turnbull, Pearl Bates, Rob Dreaming, Frances Barker, Lisa Sugden, Jez Hughes, Chrissie Weedall, Jim Fortey, Jarda Dokoupil, and so many others...

I owe specific thanks to three people who read the first draft and acted as proof-readers and informal editors to help me refine the text: Clare Myatt, Michelle Gallant, and Pearl Bates. Thank you for your time and assistance you guys (any remaining literary gaffs are mine alone!).

Author Profile

Francis trained originally as an actor, then ran away from the circus to find his home. He has studied a wide range of martial arts over the years from many continents and has a 3rd Dan black belt in Kodo Ryu Karate. It was in the world of the martial arts that he first encountered Taoism.

These days he is a workshop leader, facilitator and Interfaith Minister. He particularly enjoys facilitating The Samurai Game® (originally created by George Leonard) for which he is currently the only certified facilitator in the UK. He offers workshops and trainings around spirituality, the warrior archetype, and learning to be more present. He specialises in somatic (working with the body), and experiential training methods.

He lives in Brighton, UK with his wife and son. Francis loves the sea especially in the Autumn when it's stormy and dramatic.

If you'd like to know more about his work, find some free resources, do an online course or read Francis' blog go to:

www.fudoshin.org.uk

Warriors of Love Publishing

Warriors of Love Publishing is a branch of Fudoshin Development. We are looking to produce new works on personal and spiritual development. We are passionate about human potential, spiritual growth and books! We want to publish work that will help encourage the kind of shift in consciousness that is sorely needed to repair the relationship between human beings, other human beings, and Mother Earth.

It may seem a joke to say we are passionate about books, but it's true. We love books. Not just as repositories of knowledge and catalysts of understanding but as objects. There's something wonderful about books that e-books, e-readers, and the Kindle will never replace.

If you'd like to make orders over 5 copies in the UK or want to get in touch, go to www.fudoshin.org.uk

Lightning Source UK Ltd.
Milton Keynes UK
UKOW052031090713

213518UK00002B/366/P

9 780956 779908